# Scott Foresman
# Science
## The Diamond Edition

PEARSON
Scott
Foresman

Editorial Offices: Glenview, Illinois • Parsippany, New Jersey • New York, New York
Sales Offices: Boston, Massachusetts • Duluth, Georgia • Glenview, Illinois
Coppell, Texas • Sacramento, California • Mesa, Arizona
www.pearsonsuccessnet.com

# Series Authors

**Dr. Timothy Cooney**
*Professor of Earth Science and Science Education*
University of Northern Iowa (UNI)
Cedar Falls, Iowa

**Dr. Jim Cummins**
*Professor*
Department of Curriculum, Teaching, and Learning
University of Toronto
Toronto, Canada

**Dr. James Flood**
*Distinguished Professor of Literacy and Language*
School of Teacher Education
San Diego State University
San Diego, California

**Barbara Kay Foots, M.Ed.**
*Science Education Consultant*
Houston, Texas

**Dr. M. Jenice Goldston**
*Associate Professor of Science Education*
Department of Elementary Education Programs
University of Alabama
Tuscaloosa, Alabama

**Dr. Shirley Gholston Key**
*Associate Professor of Science Education*
Instruction and Curriculum Leadership Department
College of Education
University of Memphis
Memphis, Tennessee

**Dr. Diane Lapp**
*Distinguished Professor of Reading and Language Arts in Teacher Education*
San Diego State University
San Diego, California

**Sheryl A. Mercier**
*Classroom Teacher*
Dunlap Elementary School
Dunlap, California

**Karen L. Ostlund, Ph.D.**
*UTeach Specialist*
College of Natural Sciences
The University of Texas at Austin
Austin, Texas

**Dr. Nancy Romance**
*Professor of Science Education & Principal Investigator*
NSF/IERI Science IDEAS Project
Charles E. Schmidt College of Science
Florida Atlantic University
Boca Raton, Florida

**Dr. William Tate**
*Chair and Professor of Education and Applied Statistics*
Department of Education
Washington University
St. Louis, Missouri

**Dr. Kathryn C. Thornton**
*Former NASA Astronaut Professor*
School of Engineering and Applied Science
University of Virginia
Charlottesville, Virginia

**Dr. Leon Ukens**
*Professor Emeritus*
Department of Physics, Astronomy, and Geosciences
Towson University
Towson, Maryland

**Steve Weinberg**
*Consultant*
Connecticut Center for Advanced Technology
East Hartford, Connecticut

ISBN–13: 978-0-328-28958-5 (SVE), ISBN–10: 0-328-28958-2 (SVE);
ISBN–13: 978-0-328-30434-9 (A), ISBN–10: 0-328-30434-4 (A);
ISBN–13: 978-0-328-30435-6 (B), ISBN–10: 0-328-30435-2 (B);
ISBN–13: 978-0-328-30436-3 (C), ISBN–10: 0-328-30436-0 (C);
ISBN–13: 978-0-328-30437-0 (D), ISBN–10: 0-328-30437-9 (D)

Copyright © 2008 Pearson Education, Inc.

All Rights Reserved. Printed in the United States of America. This publication is protected by Copyright, and permission should be obtained from the publisher prior to any prohibited reproduction, storage in a retrieval system, or transmission in any form by any means, electronic, mechanical, photocopying, recording, or otherwise. For information regarding permission(s), write to: Permissions Department, Scott Foresman, 1900 East Lake Avenue, Glenview, Illinois 60025.

10 V063 15 14 13 12 11 10

CC: N1

**Photographs**
Every effort has been made to secure permission and provide appropriate credit for photographic material. The publisher deeply regrets any omission and pledges to correct errors called to its attention in subsequent editions. Unless otherwise acknowledged, all photographs are the property of Scott Foresman, a division of Pearson Education. Photo locators denoted as follows: Top (T), Center (C), Bottom (B), Left (L), Right (R), Background (Bkgd)

# Consulting Author

### Dr. Michael P. Klentschy
*Superintendent*
El Centro Elementary School District
El Centro, California

## Science Content Consultants

### Dr. Frederick W. Taylor
*Senior Research Scientist*
Institute for Geophysics
Jackson School of Geosciences
The University of Texas at Austin
Austin, Texas

### Dr. Ruth E. Buskirk
*Senior Lecturer*
School of Biological Sciences
The University of Texas at Austin
Austin, Texas

### Dr. Cliff Frohlich
*Senior Research Scientist*
Institute for Geophysics
Jackson School of Geosciences
The University of Texas at Austin
Austin, Texas

### Brad Armosky
*McDonald Observatory*
The University of Texas at Austin
Austin, Texas

# NASA Content Consultants

### Adena Williams Loston, Ph.D.
*Chief Education Officer*
Office of the Chief Education Officer

### Clifford W. Houston, Ph.D.
*Deputy Chief Education Officer for Education Programs*
Office of the Chief Education Officer

### Frank C. Owens
*Senior Policy Advisor*
Office of the Chief Education Officer

### Deborah Brown Biggs
*Manager, Education Flight Projects Office*
Space Operations Mission Directorate, Education Lead

### Erika G. Vick
*NASA Liaison to Pearson Scott Foresman*
Education Flight Projects Office

### William E. Anderson
*Partnership Manager for Education*
Aeronautics Research Mission Directorate

### Anita Krishnamurthi
*Program Planning Specialist*
Space Science Education and Outreach Program

### Bonnie J. McClain
*Chief of Education*
Exploration Systems Mission Directorate

### Diane Schweizer
*Program Scientist*
Earth Science Education

### Deborah Rivera
*Strategic Alliances Manager*
Office of Public Affairs
NASA Headquarters

### Douglas D. Peterson
*Public Affairs Officer, Astronaut Office*
Office of Public Affairs
NASA Johnson Space Center

### Nicole Cloutier
*Public Affairs Officer, Astronaut Office*
Office of Public Affairs
NASA Johnson Space Center

### Dr. Jennifer J. Wiseman
*Hubble Space Scientist Program Scientist*
NASA Headquarters

# Reviewers

**Dr. Maria Aida Alanis**
Administrator
Austin ISD
Austin Texas

**Melissa Barba**
Teacher
Wesley Mathews Elementary
Miami, Florida

**Dr. Marcelline Barron**
Supervisor/K-12 Math
and Science
Fairfield Public Schools
Fairfield, Connecticut

**Jane Bates**
Teacher
Hickory Flat Elementary
Canton, Georgia

**Denise Bizjack**
Teacher Dr. N. H. Jones
Elementary
Ocala, Florida

**Latanya D. Bragg**
Teacher
Davis Magnet School
Jackson, Mississippi

**Richard Burton**
Teacher
George Buck Elementary
School 94
Indianapolis, Indiana

**Dawn Cabrera**
Teacher E.W.F. Stirrup School
Miami, Florida

**Barbara Calabro**
Teacher
Compass Rose Foundation
Ft. Myers, Florida

**Lucille Calvin**
Teacher
Weddington Math &
Science School
Greenville, Mississippi

**Patricia Carmichael**
Teacher
Teasley Middle School
Canton, Georgia

**Martha Cohn**
Teacher
An Wang Middle School
Lowell, Massachusetts

**Stu Danzinger**
Supervisor
Community Consolidated
School District 59
Arlington Heights, Illinois

**Esther Draper**
Supervisor/Science Specialist
Belair Math Science
Magnet School
Pine Bluff, Arkansas

**Sue Esser**
Teacher
Loretto Elementary
Jacksonville, Florida

**Dr. Richard Fairman**
Teacher
Antioch University
Yellow Springs, Ohio

**Joan Goldfarb**
Teacher
Indialantic Elementary
Indialantic, Florida

**Deborah Gomes**
Teacher
A J Gomes Elementary
New Bedford, Massachusetts

**Sandy Hobart**
Teacher
Mims Elementary
Mims, Florida

**Tom Hocker**
Teacher/Science Coach
Boston Latin Academy
Dorchester, Massachusetts

**Shelley Jaques**
Science Supervisor
Moore Public Schools
Moore, Oklahoma

**Marguerite W. Jones**
Teacher
Spearman Elementary
Piedmont, South Carolina

**Kelly Kenney**
Teacher
Kansas City Missouri
School District
Kansas City, Missouri

**Carol Kilbane**
Teacher
Riverside Elementary School
Wichita, Kansas

**Robert Kolenda**
Teacher
Neshaminy School District
Langhorne, Pennsylvania

**Karen Lynn Kruse**
Teacher
St. Paul the Apostle
Yonkers, New York

**Elizabeth Loures**
Teacher
Point Fermin
Elementary School
San Pedro, California

**Susan MacDougall**
Teacher
Brick Community Primary
Learning Center
Brick, New Jersey

**Jack Marine**
Teacher
Raising Horizons Quest
Charter School
Philadelphia, Pennsylvania

**Nicola Micozzi Jr.**
Science Coordinator
Plymouth Public Schools
Plymouth, Massachusetts

**Paula Monteiro**
Teacher
A J Gomes Elementary
New Bedford, Massachusetts

**Tracy Newallis**
Teacher
Taper Avenue Elementary
San Pedro, California

**Dr. Eugene Nicolo**
Supervisor, Science K-12
Moorestown School District
Moorestown, New Jersey

**Jeffry Pastrak**
School District of Philadelphia
Philadelphia, Pennslyvania

**Helen Pedigo**
Teacher
Mt. Carmel Elementary
Huntsville Alabama

**Becky Peltonen**
Teacher
Patterson Elementary School
Panama City, Florida

**Sherri Pensler**
Teacher/ESOL
Claude Pepper Elementary
Miami, Florida

**Virginia Rogliano**
Teacher
Bridgeview Elementary
South Charleston, West
Virginia

**Debbie Sanders**
Teacher
Thunderbolt Elementary
Orange Park, Florida

**Grethel Santamarina**
Teacher
E.W.F. Stirrup School
Miami, Florida

**Migdalia Schneider**
Teacher/Bilingual
Lindell School
Long Beach, New York

**Susan Shelly**
Teacher
Bonita Springs Elementary
Bonita Springs, Florida

**Peggy Terry**
Teacher
Madison Elementary
South Holland, Illinois

**Jane M. Thompson**
Teacher
Emma Ward Elementary
Lawrenceburg, Kentucky

**Martha Todd**
Teacher
W. H. Rhodes Elementary
Milton, Florida

**Renee Williams**
Teacher
Bloomfield Schools
Central Primary
Bloomfield, New Mexico

**Myra Wood**
Teacher
Madison Street Academy
Ocala, Florida

**Marion Zampa**
Teacher
Shawnee Mission
School District
Overland Park, Kansas

# Science

## See learning in a whole new light

# Unit A Life Science

## How do plants live in their habitats?

## Chapter 1 • All About Plants

# Chapter 2 • All About Animals

## How are animals different from each other?

# Unit A Life Science

## How do living things help each other?

## Chapter 3 • How Plants and Animals Live Together

# Chapter 4 • How Living Things Grow and Change

**How do living things grow in different ways?**

## What are Earth's natural resources?

### Chapter 5 • Earth's Land, Air, and Water

# Chapter 6 • Earth's Weather and Seasons

## How does weather change?

# Unit B Earth Science

How can people learn about the Earth long ago?

## Chapter 7 • Fossils and Dinosaurs

## What are some properties of matter?

## Chapter 8 • Properties of Matter

# Chapter 9 • Energy

## What are some kinds of energy?

# Unit C  Physical Science

**How do forces cause objects to move?**

## Chapter 10 • Forces and Motion

# Chapter 11 • Sound

## How is sound made?

# Unit D  Space and Technology

## What are some ways the Earth moves?

# Chapter 12 • Earth and Space

# Chapter 13 • Technology in Our World

**What are some ways technology helps us?**

# How to Read Science

Each chapter in your book has a page like this one. This page shows you how to use a reading skill.

## Before reading
First, read the Build Background page. Next, read the How To Read Science page. Then, think about what you already know. Last, make a list of what you already know.

## Target Reading Skill
Each page has a target reading skill. The target reading skill will help you understand what you read.

## Real-World Connection
Each page has an example of something you will learn.

## Graphic Organizer
A graphic organizer can help you think about what you learn.

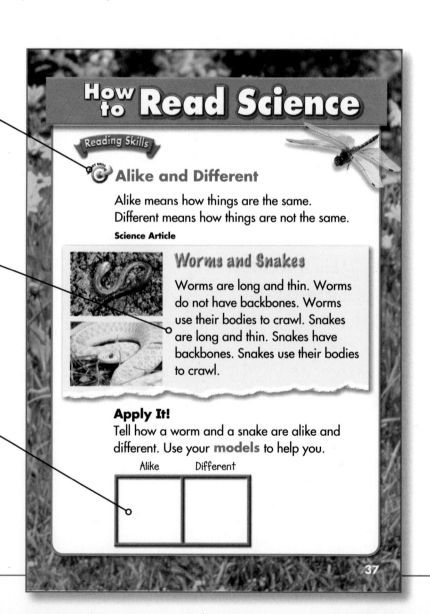

### How to Read Science

**Reading Skills**

#### Alike and Different

Alike means how things are the same. Different means how things are not the same.

**Science Article**

#### Worms and Snakes

Worms are long and thin. Worms do not have backbones. Worms use their bodies to crawl. Snakes are long and thin. Snakes have backbones. Snakes use their bodies to crawl.

**Apply It!**
Tell how a worm and a snake are alike and different. Use your **models** to help you.

| Alike | Different |
|-------|-----------|
|       |           |

**Reptiles** are animals with backbones. Most reptiles have dry skin. Scales cover and protect a reptile's body. Some reptiles hatch from eggs. Snakes and turtles are two kinds of reptiles. Look at the picture of the reptile.

**Amphibians** are animals with backbones. Amphibians live part of their life in the water and part of their life on land. Most amphibians have smooth, wet skin. Amphibians hatch from eggs. Frogs and toads are amphibians.

✓ Lesson Checkpoint

1. Which kinds of animals have backbones and scales?

2. 🔁 How are an amphibian and a reptile **alike** and **different**?

amphibian

reptile

41

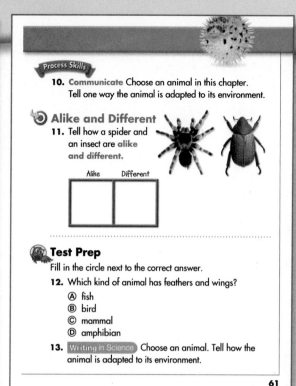

Process Skills

10. **Communicate** Choose an animal in this chapter. Tell one way the animal is adapted to its environment.

🔁 **Alike and Different**
11. Tell how a spider and an insect are **alike and different**.

| Alike | Different |
|---|---|
|  |  |

🦉 **Test Prep**
Fill in the circle next to the correct answer.

12. Which kind of animal has feathers and wings?
   Ⓐ fish
   Ⓑ bird
   Ⓒ mammal
   Ⓓ amphibian

13. Writing in Science Choose an animal. Tell how the animal is adapted to its environment.

61

🔁 **During reading**

Use the checkpoint as you read the lesson. This will help you check how much you understand.

🔁 **After reading**

Think about what you have learned. Compare what you learned with the list you made before you read the chapter. Answer the questions in the Chapter Review.

## Target Reading Skills

These are some target reading skills that appear in this book.

- Cause and Effect
- Alike and Different
- Put Things in Order
- Predict

- Draw Conclusions
- Picture Clues
- Important Details

# Science Process Skills

Scientists use process skills to find out about things. You will use these skills when you do the activities in this book. Suppose scientists want to learn more about space. Which process skills might they use?

## Observe

A scientist who wants to find out more about space observes many things. You use your senses to find out about things too.

## Classify

Scientists classify objects in space. You classify when you sort or group things by their properties.

## Estimate and Measure

Scientists build machines to explore space. First scientists make a careful guess about the size or amount of the parts of the machine. Then they measure each part.

## Infer

Scientists are always learning about space. Scientists draw a conclusion or make a guess from what they already know.

# Space

## Predict

First scientists tell what they think will happen. Then they do an experiment.

## Make and Use Models

Scientists might make and use models of a machine to use in space. Models show what scientists already know.

## Make Definitions

Scientists use what they know to tell what something means.

# Science Process Skills

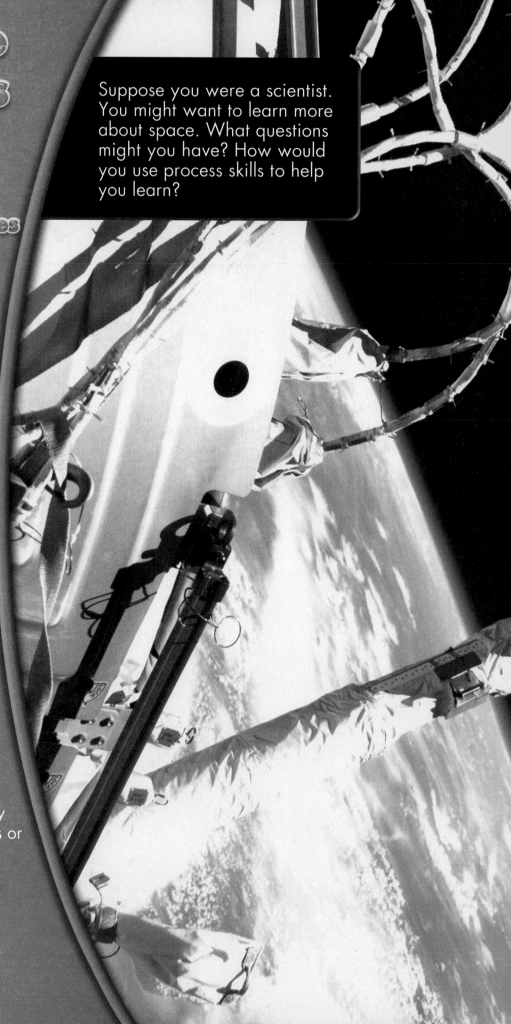

Suppose you were a scientist. You might want to learn more about space. What questions might you have? How would you use process skills to help you learn?

## Make Hypotheses
Think of a question you have about space. Make a statement that you can test to answer your question.

## Collect Data
Scientists record what they observe and measure. Scientists put this data into charts or graphs.

## Interpret Data
Scientists use what they learn to solve problems or answer questions.

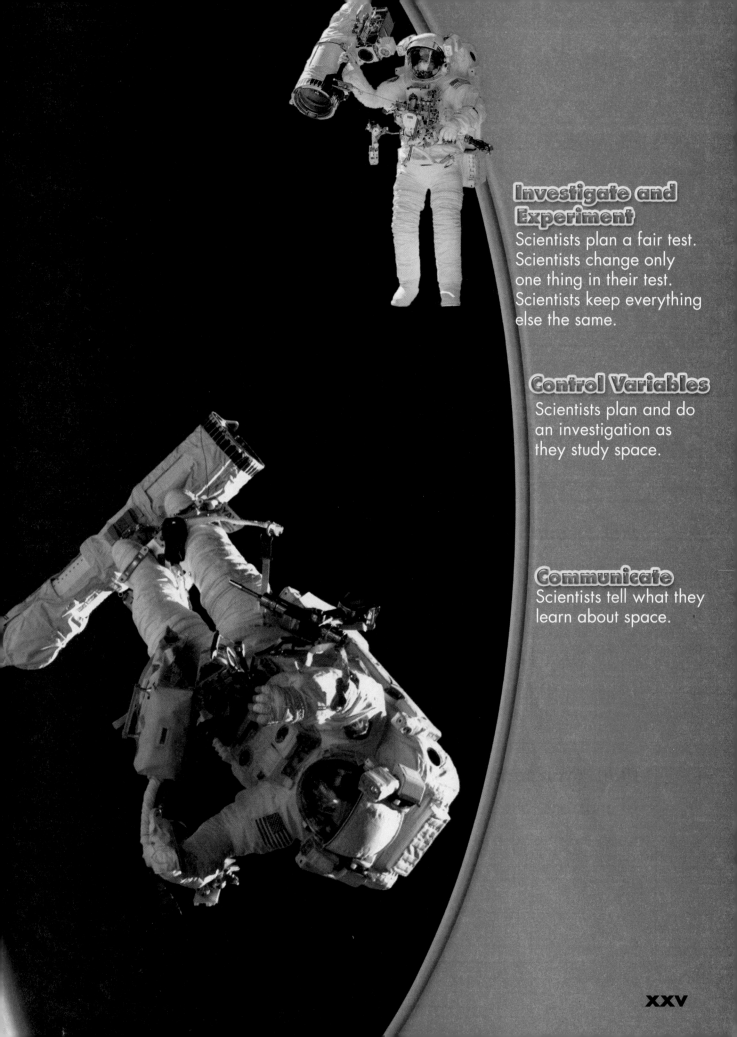

## Investigate and Experiment

Scientists plan a fair test. Scientists change only one thing in their test. Scientists keep everything else the same.

## Control Variables

Scientists plan and do an investigation as they study space.

## Communicate

Scientists tell what they learn about space.

# Using Scientific Methods

Scientific methods are ways of finding answers. Scientific methods have these steps. Sometimes scientists do the steps in a different order. Scientists do not always do all of the steps.

## Ask a question.

Ask a question that you want answered.

Do seeds need water to grow?

## Make your hypothesis.

Tell what you think the answer is to your question.

If seeds are watered, then they will grow.

## Plan a fair test.

Change only one thing.

Keep everything else the same.

Water one pot with seeds.

no water

water

## Do your test.

Test your hypothesis. Do your test more than once. See if your results are the same.

## Collect and record your data.

Keep records of what you find out. Use words or drawings to help.

## Tell your conclusion.

Observe the results of your test. Decide if your hypothesis is right or wrong. Tell what you decide.

Seeds need water to grow.

water

no water

## Go further.

Use what you learn. Think of new questions or better ways to do a test.

Ask a Question

Make Your Hypothesis

Plan a Fair Test

Do Your Test

Collect and Record Your Data

Tell Your Conclusion

Go Further

# Science Tools

Scientists use many different kinds of tools.

**Safety goggles**
You can use safety goggles to protect your eyes.

**Hand lens**
A hand lens makes objects look larger.

**Clock**
A clock measures time.

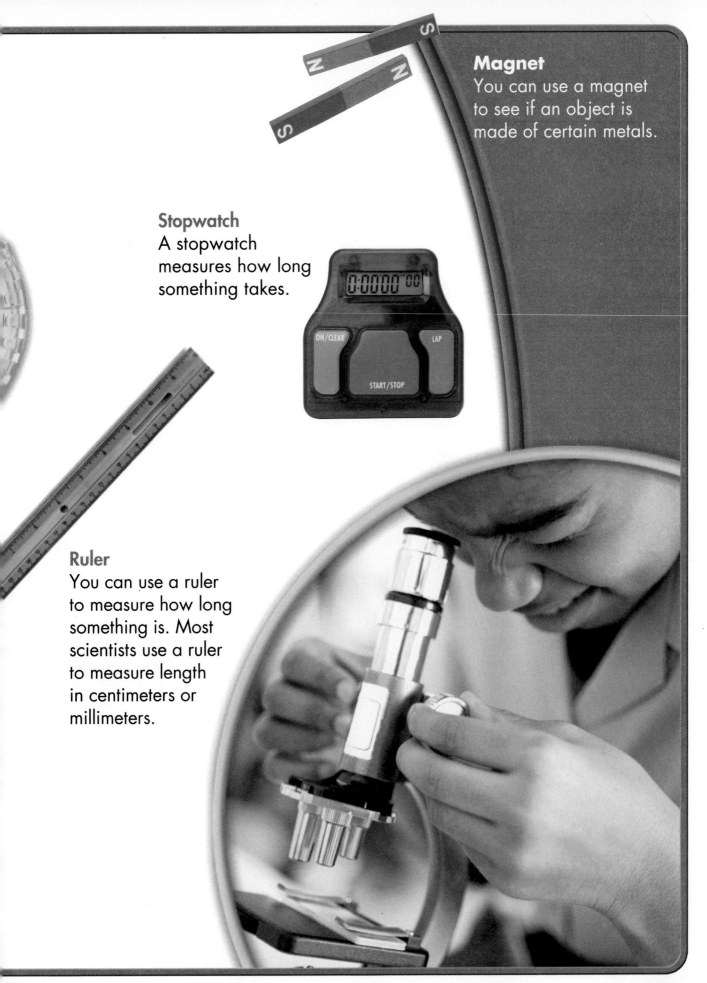

## Magnet
You can use a magnet to see if an object is made of certain metals.

## Stopwatch
A stopwatch measures how long something takes.

## Ruler
You can use a ruler to measure how long something is. Most scientists use a ruler to measure length in centimeters or millimeters.

# Science Tools

### Meterstick
You can use a meterstick to measure how long something is too. Scientists use a meterstick to measure in meters.

### Balance
A balance is used to measure the mass of objects. Mass is how much matter an object has. Most scientists measure mass in grams or kilograms.

### Measuring cup
You can use a measuring cup to measure volume. Volume is how much space something takes up.

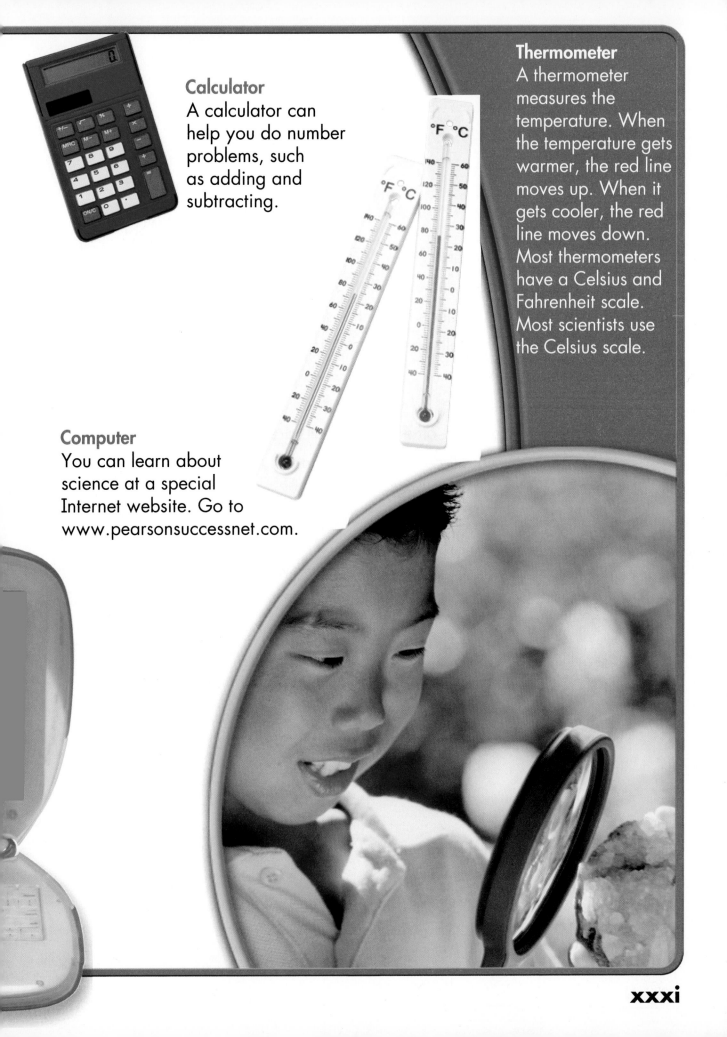

## Calculator

A calculator can help you do number problems, such as adding and subtracting.

## Thermometer

A thermometer measures the temperature. When the temperature gets warmer, the red line moves up. When it gets cooler, the red line moves down. Most thermometers have a Celsius and Fahrenheit scale. Most scientists use the Celsius scale.

## Computer

You can learn about science at a special Internet website. Go to www.pearsonsuccessnet.com.

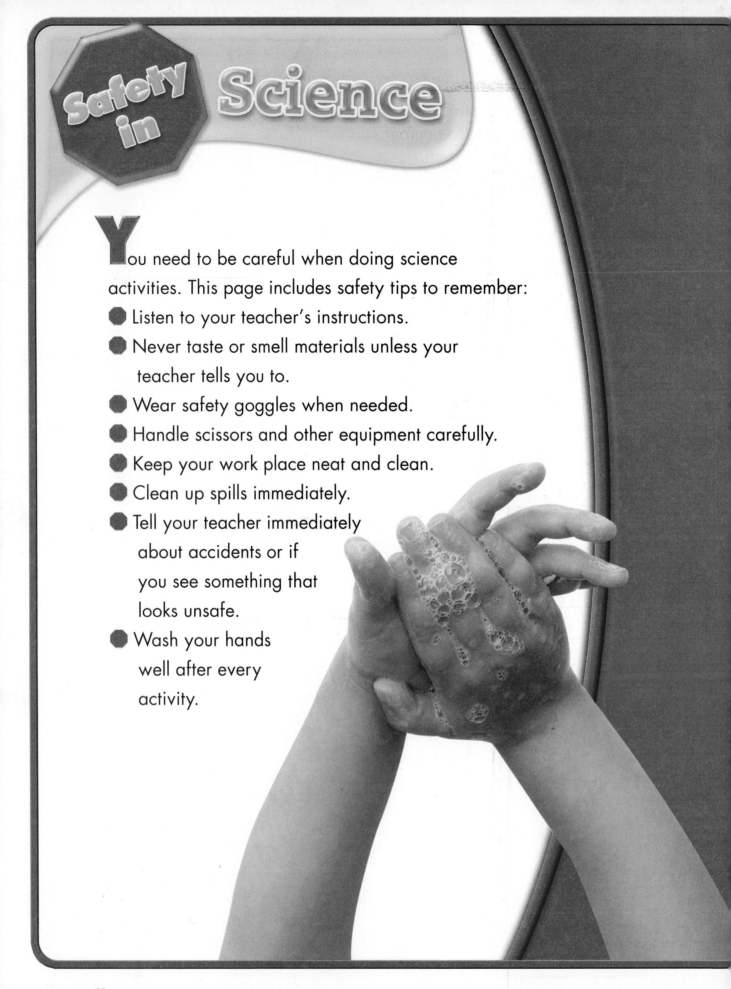

# Safety in Science

**Y**ou need to be careful when doing science activities. This page includes safety tips to remember:

- Listen to your teacher's instructions.
- Never taste or smell materials unless your teacher tells you to.
- Wear safety goggles when needed.
- Handle scissors and other equipment carefully.
- Keep your work place neat and clean.
- Clean up spills immediately.
- Tell your teacher immediately about accidents or if you see something that looks unsafe.
- Wash your hands well after every activity.

You will discover

- what is in the day and night sky.
- how Earth, the Sun, and the Moon move.

# Chapter 12
# Earth and Space

Discovery Channel School
Student DVD

DISCOVERY
CHANNEL
SCHOOL

online
Student Edition

pearsonsuccessnet.com

solar system

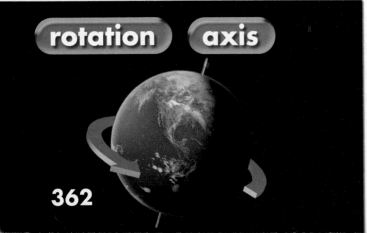

rotation  axis

constellation

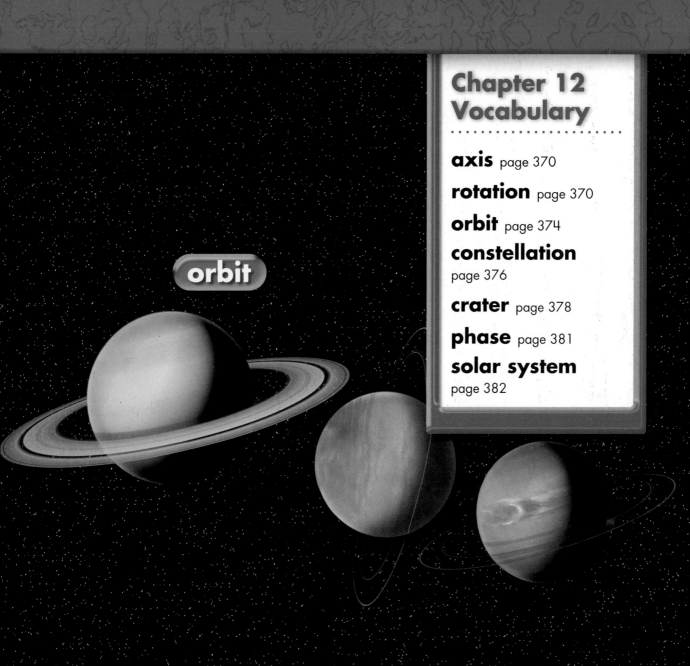

orbit

crater

phase

## Explore What causes day and night?

**Materials**

foam ball

pencil

dot sticker

crayons or markers

flashlight

## What to Do

**1** **Make a model** of Earth.

foam ball

red dot sticker

child

**2** Shine a flashlight on your model.

The flashlight is like the Sun.

**3** Turn your model of Earth. Watch the child.

## Explain Your Results
How does your **model** show day and night?

**Process Skills**

You can use **models** of Earth and the Sun to understand what causes day and night.

# How to Read Science

## Alike and Different

Alike means how things are the same.
Different means how things are not the same.

**Science Pictures**

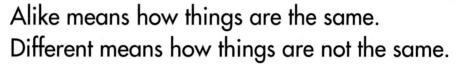

Day and Night

**Apply It!**
Look at the pictures.
Tell how day and night
are alike and different.
Think of your **model**
to help you.

| Alike | Different |
| --- | --- |
|  |  |

# The Sun

Sung to the tune of "Twinkle Twinkle Little Star"
Lyrics by Gerri Brioso & Richard Freitas/The Dovetail Group, Inc.

In the sky's a great big star.
It's the Sun and it's real far!
The Sun lights up the sky so bright.
It also lights the Moon at night.
Heat and light come from the Sun
And that is needed by everyone!

## Lesson 1
# What is the Sun?

Think of the stars you see in the sky at night. Stars are made of hot, glowing gases. The Sun is a star too. The Sun seems brighter and larger than the other stars. This is because the Sun is the closest star to Earth. The Sun is so bright that you cannot see other stars during the day.

## Why We Need the Sun

The Sun may look small, but it is really very big. The Sun is much bigger than Earth. The Sun looks small because it is so far away.

**This is what the Sun looks like in space.**

The Sun is important to Earth. Earth gets light and heat from the Sun. Living things on Earth need light and heat. People, plants, and animals can live on Earth because of the Sun.

✓ **Lesson Checkpoint**

1. Why is the Sun important to living things on Earth?

2. How are the Sun and other stars **alike** and **different?**

# What causes day and night?

The picture shows an imaginary line through
the center of Earth. This line is called an **axis.**
Earth is always spinning on its axis.
This spinning on an axis is called a **rotation.**
Earth makes one complete rotation each day.

Earth's rotation causes day and night.
When your side of Earth is facing the Sun,
you have day. When your side of Earth
is facing away from the Sun, you have night.

✓ **Checkpoint**

1. What is Earth's axis?

2. **Writing in Science** Write 2 sentences
   in your **science journal.** Tell why one
   side of Earth has day when the other
   side has night.

**It takes about
24 hours for
Earth to make
one complete
rotation.**

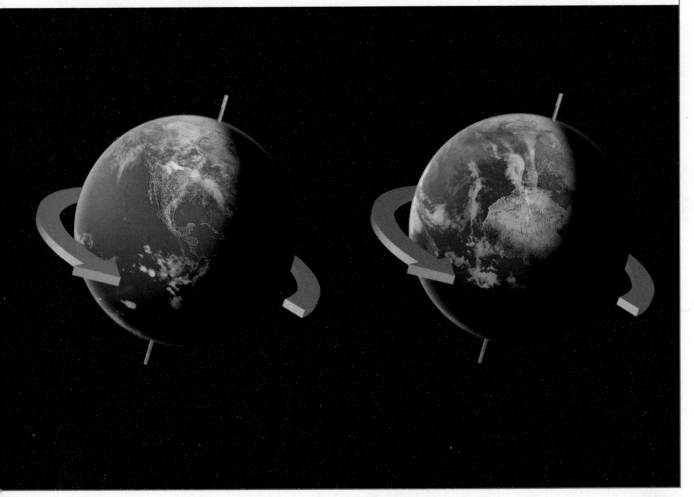

# The Sun in the Sky

The Sun seems to move across the sky during the day. The Sun looks low in the sky early in the morning. By the middle of the day, the Sun is high in the sky. In the evening, the Sun is low in the sky again.

sunrise

noon

**The Sun is always shining. The Sun is hard to see on some days.**

The Sun is not really moving across the sky. The Sun only looks like it is moving. It is really the Earth that is moving.

sunset

✓ Lesson Checkpoint

1. Why does the Sun look like it is moving across the sky?

2. **Writing in Science** Write 2 sentences in your **science journal.** Tell what time sunrise and sunset are today where you live.

# Lesson 3

# What causes seasons to change?

Earth is tilted on its axis. Earth is always tilted in the same direction.

You know that Earth spins on its axis. Earth moves around the Sun in an orbit too. An **orbit** is a path around another object.

It takes Earth about one year to orbit the Sun one time. The tilt of Earth and its orbit cause the seasons.

✓ **Lesson Checkpoint**

1. What causes the seasons?

2. **Social Studies** in Science Look at a calendar. When is the official first day of summer?

**summer**

In summer, the part of Earth where we live is tilted toward the Sun.

## spring

In spring, the part of the Earth where we live is beginning to tilt toward the Sun.

## winter

In winter, the part of Earth where we live is tilted away from the Sun.

## fall

In fall, the part of Earth where we live is beginning to tilt away from the Sun.

## Lesson 4

# What can you see in the night sky?

You can see many other stars at night. Stars in the night sky look small because they are far away. Sometimes it looks like there are more stars than you can count!

Long ago, people thought they saw patterns in some groups of stars. They imagined lines that formed pictures. A group of stars that form a picture is called a **constellation.**

This constellation looks like a lion. It is called Leo.

1. ✓Checkpoint What is a constellation?
2. Technology in Science What tools can you use to see the stars better at night?

Look at these two
constellations. They are
called the Big Dipper
and the Little Dipper.

## The Moon

You might see the Moon in the night sky too. The Moon is the largest and brightest object in the night sky.

The Moon has mountains and deep craters. A **crater** is a hole in the ground that is shaped like a bowl. A crater is formed when a large rock from space hits the Moon.

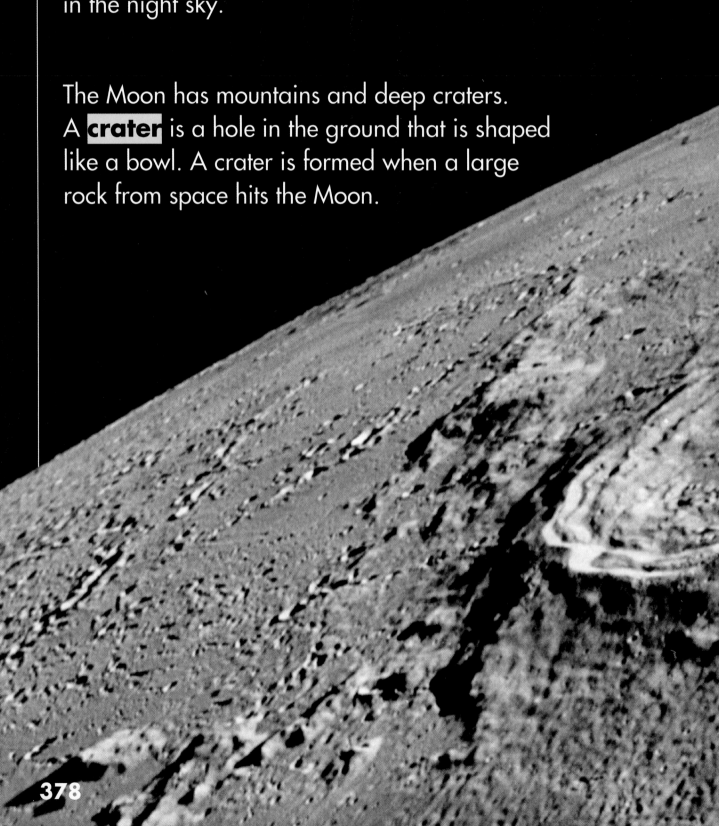

The Moon has many craters like this one.

Sometimes you can see the Moon in the daytime.

1. What causes craters on the Moon?

2. **Art in Science** Draw a picture of the clear night sky. Use chalk and dark paper.

## Lesson 5

# Why does the Moon seem to change?

The Moon rotates just like Earth. It moves in an orbit around Earth. The Moon orbits Earth while Earth orbits the Sun. It takes about four weeks for the Moon to orbit Earth one time.

**phases of the moon**

The Moon does not make its own light. The Moon reflects light from the Sun. You only see the part of the Moon that has light shining on it.

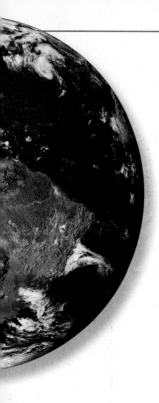

The Moon seems to change shape. Sometimes the Moon looks round. Sometimes you see smaller parts of the Moon. Sometimes you cannot see the Moon at all. The shape of the lighted part of the Moon is called a **phase.**

**The Moon is the biggest and brightest object in the night sky.**

✓ **Lesson Checkpoint**

1. Why can we see the Moon?

2. **Math in Science** How long will it take for the Moon to move around the Earth 3 times?

## Lesson 6

# What is the solar system?

Earth is a planet. You know that Earth orbits around the Sun. Other planets orbit around the Sun too. The planets and their moons and other objects that move around the Sun are called the **solar system.**

Sun

Mercury

Venus

Earth

Mars

Jupiter

The Sun is the center of our solar system. All of the objects in the solar system orbit the Sun. Count the other planets that orbit the Sun. How many planets do you count?

✓ **Lesson Checkpoint**

1. What is at the center of Earth's solar system?

2. 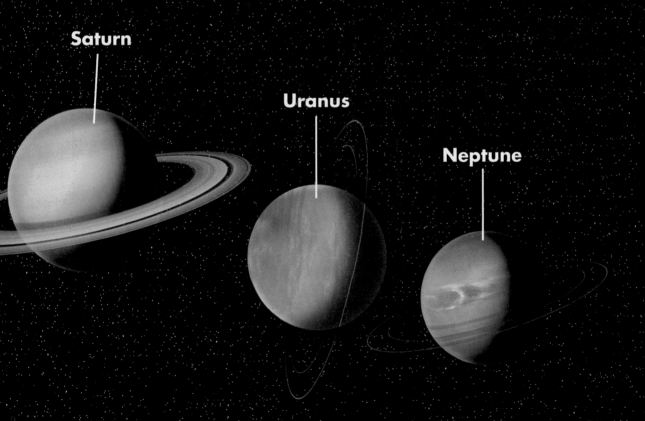 Look at the planets. Tell how they are **alike** and **different**.

**Saturn**

**Uranus**

**Neptune**

**Investigate** How can you make a model of a constellation?

## Materials

safety goggles

pencil

black paper

flashlight

## What to Do

**1** Make a **model** constellation. Poke holes through the paper with a pencil.

**2** Make the room dark. Hold the paper near a wall.

### Process Skills

You use what you learn to **make a definition** of a constellation.

More Lab zone Activities Take It to the Net
pearsonsuccessnet.com

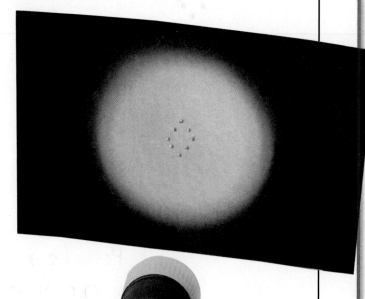

**3** Have your partner shine a flashlight on the holes in the paper. **Observe** the picture the light makes. This is your constellation.

**4** Draw and name your constellation.

**My Constellation**

## Explain Your Results

1. Tell about your constellation. How is your model like a real constellation? How is it different?

2. **Make a definition** of a constellation.

**Go Further**
How else could you make a model of your constellation? Investigate to find out.

# Planets in Orbit

Each planet takes a different number of days to orbit the Sun. This table shows how long the orbits are for some of the planets.

**Venus**

**Mercury**

**Earth**

**Mars**

**Jupiter**

| Planet | Orbit |
|--------|-------|
| Earth | 365 days |
| Mercury | 88 days |
| Venus | 225 days |
| Mars | 687 days |

1. Which of these planets takes the most number of days to orbit the Sun?

2. Which of these planets takes the fewest number of days to orbit the Sun?

3. List these planets in order from the fewest to the most number of days to orbit the Sun.

Saturn

Uranus

Neptune

Lab zone **Take-Home Activity**

Work with your family to find out how many days it takes each of the planets to orbit the Sun. Use the Internet and other resources to help you.

## Vocabulary

Which picture goes with each word?

1. axis
2. crater
3. constellation
4. orbit
5. phase
6. rotation
7. solar system

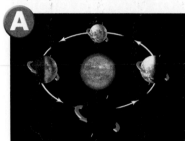

A

B

C

D

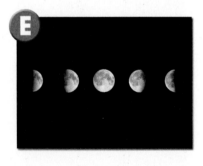

E

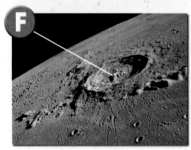

F

G

## What did you learn?

8. What is caused by Earth's rotation?
9. Why is the Sun the only star you can see during the day?

**10. Communicate** Tell why we have light during the day.

## Alike and Different

**11.** Tell how the Sun and the Moon are **alike** and **different.**

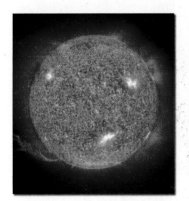

| Alike | Different |
|-------|-----------|
|       |           |

## Test Prep

Fill in the circle next to the correct answer.

**12.** Which star is closest to Earth?

Ⓐ the Sun

Ⓑ the Big Dipper

Ⓒ the Moon

Ⓓ Leo

**13.** Writing in Science Describe what you might see if you traveled around the solar system.

# Mission To Mars

NASA scientists want to learn more about the planet Mars. Mars is a planet that is close to Earth. Mars and Earth are alike in some ways. Water is needed for life on Earth. Scientists want to learn more about water on Mars.

NASA sent robots to Mars to learn about the planet. Some robots fly around Mars taking pictures. Some robots called rovers have landed on Mars. These rovers travel across the surface.

Scientists use the robots to study the environment on Mars. They take pictures of the soil and the rocks on Mars. Rovers also dig into the ground.

This rover is called *Opportunity*. *Opportunity* landed in a place called Meridiani Planum.

**Lab zone Take-Home Activity**

Suppose you are a scientist studying Mars. Write a question that you have about Mars.

# Astronomer

**Laura Peticolas is an astronomer who works with NASA. She studies natural displays of light called *auroras*. Two examples of auroras are Northern lights and Southern lights.**

## Read Together

Have you ever looked at the stars at night? People who study the Sun, stars, planets, and other things far from Earth are called astronomers.

Many astronomers use special tools called telescopes to help them see far out into space. A telescope helps things that are far away look nearer, larger, and brighter.

To study the universe, scientists at NASA launch many telescopes. One such telescope is the Hubble Space Telescope. Every day this telescope sends information to astronomers all over the world.

### Lab zone Take-Home Activity

Go outside on a clear night with your family. Look at the sky. Write about what you see.

You Will Discover

- how technology has changed the world we live in.
- ways we use technology every day.

Chapter 13

# Technology in Our World

online
**Student Edition**
pearsonsuccessnet.com

# What are some ways technology helps us?

technology

engine

vaccine

Vaccine

satellite

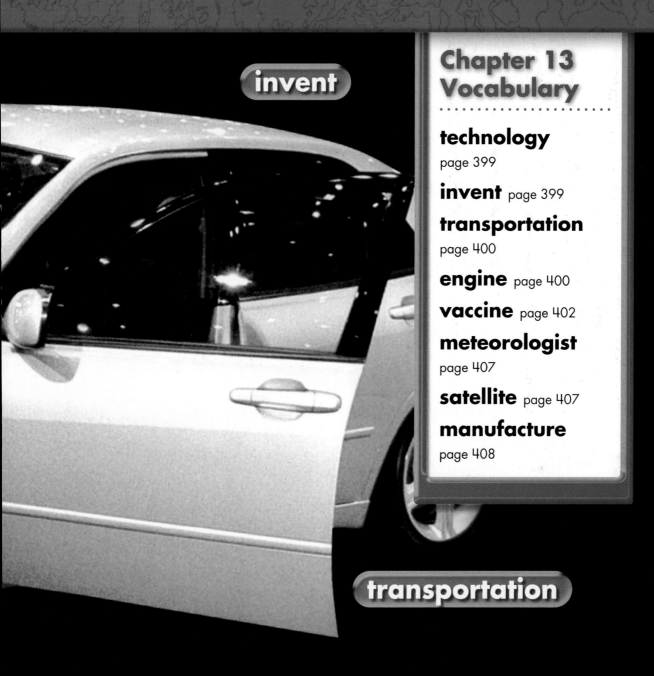

invent

transportation

manufacture

To make by hand or machine.

meteorologist

**Explore** How can you move the ball?

### Materials

metal ball

books

cup

pencil

ruler

magnet

spoon

## What to Do

**1** Put the ball on the books.
Place the cup 25 cm away
from the books.

**2** Solve this problem.
Put the ball in the cup.
Use tools.

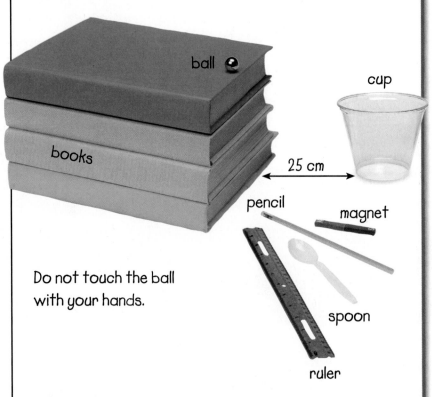

ball

books

cup

25 cm

pencil

magnet

spoon

ruler

Do not touch the ball
with your hands.

### Process Skills

When you
**communicate**,
you tell how you
moved the ball.

## Explain Your Results

**Communicate** Tell how
you solved the problem.

# How to Read Science

**TARGET SKILL** Retell

Retell means to tell what you learned in your own words.

**Science Article**

## Bicycles

The first bicycle was invented in 1817. Riders pushed their feet on the ground to make it move. Pedals were added in 1839. The pedals helped people ride bicycles with their feet off the ground.

## Apply It!
**Communicate**
Tell what you learned about bicycles.

Retell

You Are There

# Technology Helps Us All

Sung to the tune of "Bingo"
Lyrics by Gerri Brioso & Richard Freitas/The Dovetail Group, Inc.

Technology now helps us all
In lots of different ways. It
Helps us travel fast,
Helps us travel far,
Helps us travel safe,
In cars, and trains and airplanes.

Science Songs

# Lesson 1

# What is technology?

People ride in cars. People use computers. We can do these things because of technology. **Technology** means using science to help us solve problems.

Sometimes people use technology to invent things. **Invent** means to make something for the first time.

Inventions can be things we need or things we want. Many people need cars to travel long distances. Some people want computer games.

## Changes in Transportation

Technology has changed transportation. **Transportation** moves people and things from place to place. Today people travel farther and faster than they did long ago.

Some kinds of transportation have engines. An **engine** is a machine that does work or makes something move. Long ago, steam engines made trains and boats move. Today, cars, trains, and boats have gasoline or electric engines.

Technology helps people travel. Seat belts and air bags help make cars safe. Airplanes fly faster than ever before.

People use technology to help solve problems. Gasoline can cause pollution. New cars have been invented that use gasoline and electricity. These cars help reduce pollution.

✓ **Lesson Checkpoint**

1. How has technology changed transportation?

2. **Writing** in Science  Write a sentence in your **science journal.** Tell about some inventions that can help you.

# How does technology help us?

Technology can help people stay healthy. People use technology to make vaccines. A **vaccine** is a medicine that can help prevent a disease.

vaccine

Doctors use technology to help people. Glasses and contact lenses can help people to see. Hearing aids can help people to hear. Artificial legs can help some people to walk.

**The doctor uses an x ray to help this boy get well.**

**This is a picture from an MRI.**

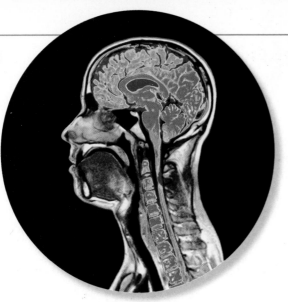

Technology can help doctors find out why people are sick. X rays, CAT scans, and MRIs are tools doctors can use to see inside people. When doctors know what is wrong, they can help people to get well.

**This man can run with the help of his artificial leg.**

✓ Lesson Checkpoint

1. What are some ways that technology can help people?

2. 🎯 **Retell** What are some tools that help doctors see inside people?

## Lesson 3

# How do we use technology to communicate?

What are some ways you communicate with your friends? The way technology is used to communicate has changed over the years.

Long ago, telephones were attached to a wall. Today you can carry a telephone with you. Telephones are much smaller today than they were years ago.

**This telephone is from 1879!**

The first computers were very big and very heavy. Today, computers are smaller, faster, and easier to use than the first computers.

**The first computer was invented in 1946. It filled a whole room!**

√ **Lesson Checkpoint**

1. How has technology changed the way people communicate?

2. Math in Science Some early telephones were about 46 centimeters tall. Today, some phones are about 9 centimeters tall. How much taller were older telephones than newer telephones?

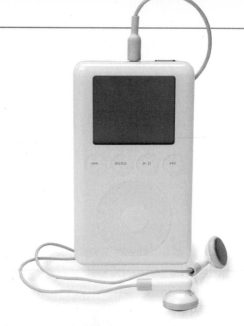

## Lesson 4

# What are some other ways we use technology?

Technology has changed the way people have fun. People listen to music on compact discs. People use computers to play games.

**MP3 players play music.**

Technology can also make our lives easier. People use Velcro® to close things. People use calculators to do math.

**Electricity can control the loudness of some guitars.**

Technology helps people in their jobs. A **meteorologist** is a person who studies weather. Meteorologists study pictures taken by satellites to predict weather. A **satellite** is an object that revolves around another object.

Satellites send information about the weather to Earth.

Meteorologists get information about the weather from satellites.

✓ Lesson Checkpoint

1. How does a meteorologist use information from satellites?

2. Writing in Science Write a sentence in your **science journal.** Tell three ways you used technology today.

**Lesson 5**

# How do people make things?

People manufacture things we use every day. **Manufacture** means to make by hand or by machines. Coats and bicycles are two things that are manufactured.

**Natural materials were used to make parts of this coat.**

Different types of materials are used to manufacture things. Some materials come from nature. This coat was made using wool from sheep. The buttons were made from wood.

Some materials are made by people. The seat of this bicycle is made from plastic. The tires are made from rubber. Plastic and rubber are materials made by people.

**This bike uses materials made by people.**

✓ Lesson Checkpoint

1. What are some manufactured things you use in school?

2. **Retell** What are some materials used to make a bicycle?

## Investigate How can you make a maze?

### Materials

safety goggles

marble

cardboard

paper tubes

box

tape and scissors

### What to Do

**1** How can you make a maze that a marble can follow? Make a plan. Draw it.

**2** Tape paper tubes to the cardboard.

**3** **Predict** Will your maze work?

**4** Test your maze. **Observe** the marble. Move the tubes to make the maze work better.

**Process Skills**

You **predict** when you tell what you think will happen.

**5** Test your maze 2 more times.

Your maze might look like this one.

| Test your maze. | |
|---|---|
| **Test** | **Did the marble follow the maze?** |
| 1 | |
| 2 | |
| 3 | |

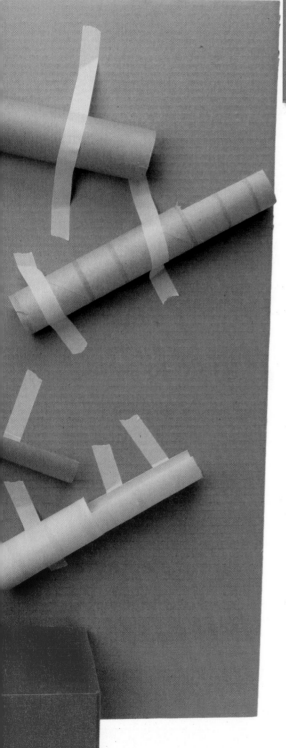

Be sure
to wear your
safety goggles.

## Explain Your Results
**Communicate** Tell how the parts of your maze work together.

### Go Further

How can you make your marble move in a different way? Investigate to find out.

# Technology in Your School

Look around your school. How many things can you find that help people communicate? How many things can you find that help people move from place to place? Fill in your table with examples.

## Technology in My School

| Communication | Transportation |
| --- | --- |
|  |  |

1. Count the examples you found for each column.
2. Compare the number of examples you found. Use <, >, or =.

**Lab zone** **Take-Home Activity**

Walk around your home. Look for ways you use technology. Make a table like the one you made for your school.

413

## Vocabulary

Which picture goes with each word?

1. engine
2. vaccine
3. satellite
4. meteorologist

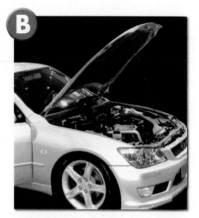

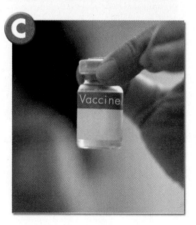

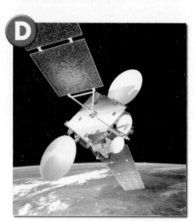

## What did you learn?

5. What is technology?

6. Name two ways you use technology every day.

7. How has technology changed communication?

**8. Infer** Why do people invent new things?

## ⟳ Retell

9. Tell what you learned about toothbrushes.

Retell

The first toothbrush was invented in China in the 1400s. The bristles were made from animal hair. The first electric toothbrush was invented in 1960. Today, bristles are made from nylon.

## 🦉 Test Prep

Fill in the circle next to the correct answer.

10. What is an object that travels around another object?

   Ⓐ engine
   Ⓑ vaccine
   Ⓒ satellite
   Ⓓ velcro

11. **Writing in Science** Make a list. Tell how people use technology.

415

# Meet Shonte Wright

Shonte Wright traveled across the United States with five other scientists. They told people about the rovers that landed on Mars in 2004.

## Read Together

In 2004 NASA sent two robots to Mars. The robots were called rovers. The rovers took pictures of Mars and sent them back to Earth. NASA used the pictures to study the planet.

Shonte Wright is one of the scientists who worked with NASA on the rovers. She helped make sure the rovers would still work after the long trip through space.

Ms. Wright knew she wanted to be a scientist and work at NASA when she was ten years old. She took many math and science classes to help her get ready for her job.

### Lab zone Take-Home Activity

Suppose you are going to invent a robot to explore another planet. Draw what the robot would look like.

**Test-Taking Strategies**

Find Important Words

Choose the Right Answer

Use Information from Text and Graphics

▶ Write Your Answer

## Write Your Answer

You can write your answer to science questions. Remember that your answer should be short but complete.

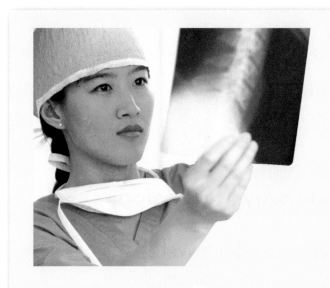

Doctors use technology to help you when you are sick or hurt. They can use X-ray, CAT scan, or an MRI to see inside your body. Best of all, using these machines doesn't hurt!

Read the question. Look at the text.

Why does a doctor use X-ray or CAT scan technology?

Which words can you use to help write your answer? Write your answer.

# Unit D Wrap-Up

**Chapter 12**

## What are some ways the Earth moves?
- Earth is always spinning on its axis.
- Earth moves around the Sun in an orbit.

**Chapter 13**

## What are some ways technology helps us?
- Technology helps people travel, communicate, and make things.
- Doctors use technology to help people get well.

## Performance Assessment

### Make a Technology Collage

- Find pictures of people using technology to communicate.

- Cut out the pictures.

- Make a collage.

- Tell about the pictures you found.

## Read More About Space & Technology!

Look for books like these in your library.

# Experiment Which tissue is the strongest?

Tissues can be strong or weak. Experiment to find out which tissue is the strongest. The tissue that holds the most water is the strongest.

## Materials

3 tissues

jar and rubber band

dropper and cup with water

marbles

balance

gram cubes

### Process Skills

You **collect data** when you use a chart to record your data.

## Ask a question.
Are tissues that cost more stronger than tissues that cost less?

## Make a hypothesis.
If a tissue costs the most, then it is the strongest.

## Plan a fair test.
Use the same amount of water to wet each tissue. Use 3 different brands of tissue.

## Do your test.

1 Put a tissue on the jar. Put a rubber band around it.

2 Wet the tissue drop by drop. Use 30 drops.

**3** Carefully place one marble at a time on top of the tissue.

**4** Count how many marbles it takes to break the tissue.

**5** **Measure** the mass of the marbles.

**6** Repeat with the other tissues.

## Collect and record data.

| Tissue Cost | How many marbles? | How many grams? |
|---|---|---|
| Most | | |
| Middle | | |
| Least | | |

## Tell your conclusion.
Which tissue is the strongest?

### Go Further
What if you used less water to wet each tissue? Try it and find out.

# This Happy Day

by Harry Behn

Every morning when the Sun
Comes smiling up on everyone,
It's lots of fun
To say good morning to the Sun.
Good morning, Sun!

Every evening after play
When the sunshine goes away,
It's nice to say,
Thank you for this happy day,
This happy day!

**Using Scientific Methods**
1. Ask a question.
2. Make a hypothesis.
3. Plan a fair test.
4. Do your test.
5. Collect and record data.
6. Tell your conclusion.
7. Go further.

### Idea 1
## Phases of the Moon

Plan a project. Find out what the Moon looks like every day for one month.

### Idea 2
## Flying Better

Make a plan. Find out if changing the size of a helicopter's blades will make it fly better.

# Metric and Customary Measurement

Science uses the metric system to measure things. Metric measurement is used around the world. Here is how different metric measurements compare to customary measurement.

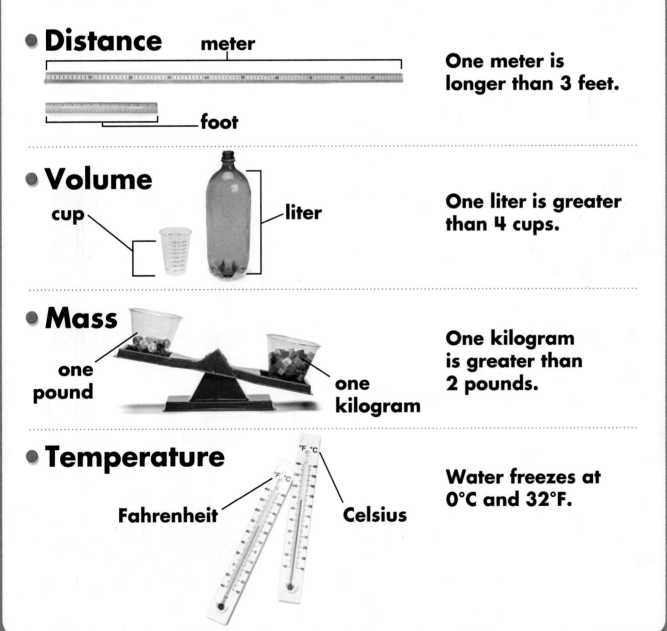

- **Distance**

meter

foot

One meter is longer than 3 feet.

- **Volume**

cup

liter

One liter is greater than 4 cups.

- **Mass**

one pound

one kilogram

One kilogram is greater than 2 pounds.

- **Temperature**

Fahrenheit

Celsius

Water freezes at 0°C and 32°F.

# Glossary

The glossary uses letters and signs to show how words are pronounced. The mark ′ is placed after a syllable with a primary or heavy accent. The mark ′ is placed after a syllable with a secondary or lighter accent.

To hear these words pronounced, listen to the AudioText CD.

## A

**adapt** (ə dapt′) To change. Animals are **adapted** to live in their environment. (page 16)

**amphibian** (am fib′ē ən) An animal with bones that lives part of its life on land and part of its life in water. My pet frog is an **amphibian.** (page 41)

**attract** (ə trakt′) To pull toward. The opposite poles of two magnets will **attract** one another. (page 318)

**axis** (ak′sis) An imaginary line around which a planet turns. Earth spins on an **axis.** (page 370)

## B

**bird** (bėrd) An animal with a backbone that has feathers, two legs, and wings. The **bird** flew from place to place searching for food. (page 40)

**boulder** (bōl′der) A very big rock. The **boulder** is by the water. (page 146)

## C

**camouflage** (kam′ə fläzh) A color or shape that makes a plant or an animal hard to see. Some animals use **camouflage** to hide themselves from danger. (page 42)

**condense** (kən dens′) To change from a gas to a liquid. Water vapor **condenses** on the outside of my glass of juice. (page 179)

**conductor** (kən duk′tər) Something that lets heat easily move through it. Metal is a **conductor.** (page 281)

**constellation** (kon′sta lā′shen) A group of stars that form a picture. I like to search the night sky for **constellations.** (page 376)

**consumer** (kən sü′mər) A living thing that cannot make its own food. Animals are **consumers.** (page 71)

**crater** (krā′tər) A hole that is shaped like a bowl. There are many **craters** on the surface of the Moon. (page 378)

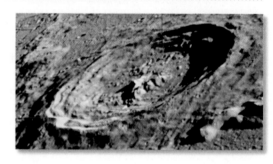

## D

**dinosaur** (dī′nə sôr) An extinct animal that lived millions of years ago. **Dinosaurs** are large animals that lived on Earth long ago. (page 212)

## E

**energy** (en′ər jē) The ability to do work or make change. You need **energy** to play soccer. (page 271)

**engine** (en′jən) A machine that changes energy into force or motion. Cars, trains, and airplanes have an **engine** that helps them run. (page 400)

**environment** (en vī′rən mənt) Everything that surrounds a living thing. A cactus is a plant that grows in a desert **environment.** (page 16)

**erosion** (i rō′zhən) Process by which rocks and soil are moved from one place to another. Heavy rains can cause **erosion.** (page 152)

**evaporate** (i vap′ ə rāt) To change from a liquid to a gas. The puddle of water will **evaporate** and turn into water vapor. (page 179)

**extinct** (ek stingkt′) An animal or plant no longer living on Earth. Dinosaurs are **extinct.** (page 210)

**fish** (fish) An animal with bones that lives in water and has gills. Many types of **fish** live in an ocean. (page 40)

**flower** (flou′ər) The part of a plant that makes seeds. Some plants have many **flowers.** (page 9)

**food chain** (füd chān) Plants use sunlight, air, and water to make food. Animals eat the plants. Other animals eat those animals. This is called a food chain. A coyote and a mountain lion are part of a **food chain.** (page 74)

**food web** (füd web) A food web is made up of the food chains in a habitat. Corn, voles, and coyotes are part of a **food web.** (page 76)

**force** (fôrs) A push or pull that makes something move. You use **force** to move the wagon. (page 304)

**fossil** (fos′əl) A print or remains of a plant or animal that lived long ago. Dinosaur **fossils** are in the museum. (page 207)

**friction** (frik′shən) A force that slows down or stops moving objects. A bicycle's brakes use **friction** to slow down. (page 312)

**fuel** (fyü′əl) Anything that is burned to make heat or power. We use wood as **fuel**. (page 279)

**G**

**gas** (gas) Matter that always takes the size and shape of its container. Bubbles are filled with **gas.** (page 246)

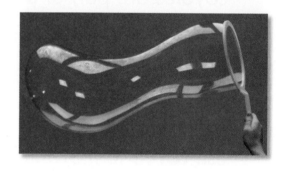

**germinate** (jėr′mə nāt) To begin to grow into a young plant. The plant seeds will soon **germinate.** (page 114)

**gills** (gilz) Special body parts that get oxygen from water. Fish have **gills**. (page 46)

**gravity** (grav′ə tē) A force that pulls things toward the center of Earth. **Gravity** will pull the leaves back to Earth. (page 306)

**hibernate** (hī′bər nāt) To spend all winter sleeping or resting. Some animals **hibernate**. (page 186)

**hurricane** (hėr′ə kān) A storm that starts over warm ocean waters that has hard rain and very strong winds. A **hurricane** causes heavy rain and strong winds. (page 192)

**insect** (in′sekt) An animal without bones that has three body parts and six legs. It's fun to watch **insects.** (page 52)

**invent** (in vent´) To make something for the first time. Alexander Graham Bell **invented** the telephone. (page 399)

**leaves** (lēvz) Parts of a plant that use sunlight, air, nutrients, and water to make food for the plant. The **leaves** on the plant are long and thin. (page 8)

**life cycle** (līf sī´kəl) The way a living thing grows and changes. We studied the **life cycle** of a turtle. (page 106)

**lightning** (līt´ning) A flash of electricity in the sky. We watched **lightning** flash across the sky. (page 188)

**liquid** (lik′wid) Matter that does not have its own shape, but does have its own mass. **Liquids** take the shape of their containers. (page 244)

**loudness** (loud′nəs) How loud or soft a sound is. The **loudness** of some sounds can change. (page 336)

**M**

**mammal** (mam′əl) An animal with bones that usually has hair or fur on its body and feeds milk to its young. Chipmunks are **mammals.** (page 40)

**manufacture** (man′yə fak′chər) To make by hand or machine. Many countries in the world **manufacture** clothing. (page 408)

**mass** (mas) The amount of matter in an object. I use a balance to measure **mass.** (page 239)

**meteorologist** (mē′tē ə rol′ə jist) A person who studies weather. The **meteorologist** predicted sunny weather. (page 407)

**migrate** (mī′grāt) To move from one place to another in a regular pattern. Many types of birds **migrate** in the winter. (page 184)

**mineral** (min′ər əl) A nonliving solid that comes from Earth. Copper is a **mineral.** (page 147)

**mixture** (miks′chər) Something made up of two or more kinds of matter that do not change. Fruit salad is a **mixture** of different fruits. (page 250)

**motion** (mō′shen) Motion is the act of moving. A merry-go-round moves in a circular **motion.** (page 303)

N

**natural resource** (nach′ər əl rē′sôrs) A useful thing that comes from nature. Rocks are **natural resources.** (page 143)

**nutrients** (nü′trē ənt) Materials that living things need to live and grow. People get **nutrients** from the food they eat. (page 7)

**nymph** (nimf) A young insect that looks like its parent and grows wings as it changes. We found a dragonfly **nymph** in the pond by our school. (page 108)

**orbit** (ôr′bit) The path around something. It takes Earth about one year to orbit the Sun one time. (page 374)

**paleontologist** (pā′lē on tol′ə jist) A scientist who studies fossils. **Paleontologists** study fossils to learn about life long ago. (page 207)

**phase** (fāz) The shape of the lighted part of the Moon. The Moon's **phases** can be seen best at night. (page 381)

**pitch** (pich) How high or low a sound is. The sound from the bullfrog had a low **pitch.** (page 338)

**pollution** (pə lü′ shən) Anything harmful added to land, air, or water. Many people work hard to reduce **pollution.** (page 154)

**prairie** (prâr′ē) Flat land covered with grasses and having few trees. A **prairie** has a lot of grass and few trees. (page 20)

**predator** (pred′ə tər) An animal that catches and eats another animal for food. A lion is a **predator.** (page 75)

**prey** (prā) An animal that is caught and eaten for food. Sea stars are the **prey** of sea otters. (page 75)

**producer** (prə dü′sər) A living thing that makes its own food. A kelp is a **producer.** (page 71)

**property** (prop′ər tē) Something about an object that you can observe with your senses. An object's color is one kind of **property.** (page 240)

**recycle** (rē sī′kəl) To change something so that it can be used again. My family **recycles** plastic bottles. (page 156)

**reflect** (ri flekt′) To bounce off of something. A mirror can **reflect** light. (page 282)

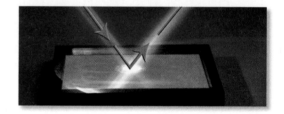

**repel** (ri pel′) To push away. The north ends of magnets will **repel** one another. (page 318)

**reptile** (rep′tīl) An animal with bones that has dry, scaly skin. Snakes are **reptiles.** (page 41)

**roots** (rüts) Parts of a plant that hold the plant in place and that take in water and nutrients from the soil. The **roots** of the old oak tree are deep inside the ground. (page 8)

**rotation** (rō tā′shən) Spinning on an axis. Earth makes one complete **rotation** each day. (page 370)

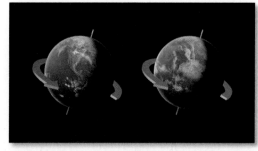

**S**

**sand** (sand) Tiny pieces of rock. People use **sand** to build roads. (page 146)

**satellite** (sat′l īt) An object that revolves around another object. Meteorologists study pictures taken by **satellites** to predict weather. (page 407)

**seed coat** (sēd kōt) The hard outer covering of a seed. The **seed coat** protects the seed. (page 114)

**seedling** (sēd′ling) A young plant. The tree **seedling** grows into a tree. (page 114)

**shadow** (shad′ō) A shadow is made when something blocks the light. The tree makes a **shadow.** (page 284)

**simple machine** (sim′pəl mə shēn) A tool with few or no moving parts that makes work easier. Workers often use **simple machines** to help them build things. (page 314)

**solar energy** (sō′lər en′ərjē) Solar energy is heat and light from the Sun. The house is heated by **solar energy.** (page 272)

**solar system** (sō′lər sis′tem) The Sun, the planets and their moons, and other objects that orbit the Sun. Earth is in our **solar system.** (page 382)

**solid** (sol′id) Matter that has its own shape and takes up space. The case that hold the supplies is a **solid.** (page 242)

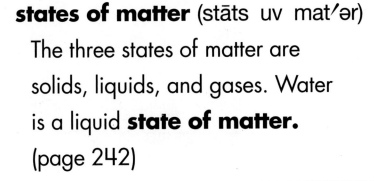

**source** (sôrs) A place from which something comes. A lamp is one **source** of light. (page 278)

**states of matter** (stāts uv mat′ər) The three states of matter are solids, liquids, and gases. Water is a liquid **state of matter.** (page 242)

**stem** (stem) Part of a plant that holds it up and that carries water and nutrients to the leaves. The **stem** is long and green. (page 8)

**technology** (tek nol′ə jē) Using
science to help solve problems.
People use **technology**
every day. (page 399)

**tornado** (tôr nā′ dō) Very strong
wind that comes down from
clouds in the shape of a funnel. A
**tornado** touched down near our
town. (page 190)

**transportation** (tran′spər tā′ shən)
Ways to move people or things
from place to place. Today,
**transportation** makes travel
easier and faster than ever before.
(page 400)

**vaccine** (vak sēn′) Medicine
that can help prevent a disease.
Mia got a shot of the flu **vaccine.**
(page 402)

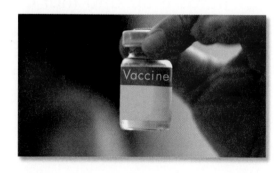

**vibrate** (vī′brāt) To move back and forth very fast. A flute makes the air **vibrate** to make sounds. (page 335)

**water cycle** (wȯ′tər sī′kəl) The way water moves from the clouds to Earth and back to the clouds. Water condenses and evaporates during the **water cycle.** (page 178)

**weathering** (weṮH′ər ing) The breaking apart and changing of rocks. **Weathering** causes sharp rocks to become smooth. (page 153)

**work** (wėrk) When force moves an object. It took a lot of **work** to push the sled up the hill. (page 308)

# Index

This Index lists the pages on which topics appear in this book. Page numbers after a *p* refer to a photograph. Page numbers after a *c* refer to a chart or graph.

# Credits

## Text

"Little Seeds" from *The Winds that Come From Far Away and Other Poems* by Else Holmelund Minarik. Copyright ©1964 by Else Holmelund Minarik. Used by permission of HarperCollins Publishers.

"The Spring Wind" from *River Winding: Poems* by Charolotte Zolotow; Copyright ©1970 by Charlotte Zolotow. Reprinted by permission of S©ott Treimel, NY.

"This Happy Day" from *The Little Hill* by Harry Behn (Harcourt Brace, 1949).

"Apple Shadows" reprinted from *Black Earth, Gold Sun* by Patricia Hubbell with permission of Marshall Cavendish. Copyright ©2001 by Cavendish Children's Books.

## Illustrations

29, 301, 327, 362, 367–368, 370–374, 376, 378, 380, 382, 388 Bob Kayganich; 69 Patrick Gnan; 201–203, 205-208 Big Sesh Studios; 344 Philip Williams; 365 Mary Teichman.

## Photographs

Every effort has been made to secure permission and provide appropriate credit for photographic material. The publisher deeply regrets any omission and pledges to correct errors called to its attention in subsequent editions.

Unless otherwise acknowledged, all photographs are the property of Scott Foresman, a division of Pearson Education.

Photo locators denoted as follows: Top (T), Center (C), Bottom (B), Left (L), Right (R), Background (Bkgd).

**Cover:** (C) ©Chase Swift/Corbis, (B) ©Walter Hodges/Corbis, (Bkgd) ©Ralph A. Clevenger/Corbis, (Bkgd) ©George Grall/NGS Image Collection

**Title Page:** ©Tom Brakefield/Corbis

**Front Matter:** ii ©DK Images; iii (TR, BR) ©DK Images; v ©DK Images; vi (CL) ©David Middleton/NHPA Limited, (CL) ©Stephen Dalton/NHPA Limited; vii (CR) Tom Brakefield/Corbis, (B) Geoff Moon; Frank Lane Picture Agency/Corbis; viii (CL) Nigel J. Dennis/NHPA Limited, (B) William Bernard/Corbis; ix Andy Rouse/NHPA Limited; x (CL) ©Stone/Getty Images, (CL) ©Steve Terrill/Corbis, (B) ©DK Images; xi ©Jim Zuckerman/Corbis; xiii ©DK Images; xiv ©Charles Gupton/Corbis; xv ©Kelly-Mooney Photography/Corbis; xvi (CL) ©Lester Lefkowitz/Corbis, (CL) Getty Images; xvii (CR) ©John Gillmoure/Corbis, (Bkgd) ©Handout/Reuters/Corbis; xviii (CL, B) NASA Image Exchange, (CL) Getty Images, (BC) ©NASA/JPL/Handout/Reuters/Corbis; xix ©Reuters/Corbis; xxiv NASA; xxv Getty Images; xxix ©Royalty-Free/Corbis; xxxi ©Ed Bock/Corbis.

**Unit A: Divider:** (Bkgd) Digital Vision, (CC) Digital Vision; **Chapter 1:** 1 (C) ©David Middleton/NHPA Limited, (BR) ©Stephen Dalton/NHPA Limited, (TR) Brand X Pictures; 2 (BR) ©DK Images, (T) Corbis; 3 (BL) ©DK Images, (BR) Richard Hamilton Smith/Corbis; 5 (Bkgd) Corbis, (TR) ©Stephen Dalton/NHPA Limited, (CL) ©Eric Crichton/Corbis; 6 (C) Corbis, (TR) ©Stephen Dalton/NHPA Limited; 7 (BR) Brand X Pictures, (TR) Hemera Technologies; 8 (TL, BL, BC) ©DK Images; 10 Brand X Pictures; 11 (CL) ©Ted Mead/PhotoLibrary, (TR, BR) ©DK Images, (TL) ©Michael Boys/Corbis, (CR) ©ChromaZone Images/Index Stock Imagery, (BL) ©Scott Camazine/Photo Researchers, Inc.; 12 (TL) Peter Anderson/©DK Images, (CR) ©Cosmo Condina/Getty Images; 13 (CL) Steve Kaufman/Corbis, (CR) Ted Levin/Animals Animals/Earth Scenes; 14 Getty Images; 15 (TR, CR) ©DK Images, (TL) ©Bill Ross/Corbis, (CL) ©Ed Reschke/Peter Arnold, Inc., (BL) ©Ted Mead/PhotoLibrary, (BR) Getty Images; 16 (CR) ©M.P. Kahl/DRK Photo, (TL) ©DK Images; 17 (CL)©Royalty-Free/Corbis, (TR) ©DK Images; 18 (TL) ©Medford Taylor/NGS Image Collection, (BR) ©Eric Crichton/Corbis; 19 (TR, BR) ©DK Images, (C) ©Bob Wickham/PhotoLibrary; 20 (TL) ©Pat O'Hara/Corbis, (BR) Neil Fletcher and Matthew Ward/©DK Images; 21 (C) Getty Images, (TR) ©Pat O'Hara/Corbis, (BR) ©David Muench/Corbis; 22 (BR) ©Ronald Martin, (TL) Getty Images; 23 (C) Randall Hyman Photography, (BR) ©Patti Murray/Animals Animals/Earth Scenes, (TR) ©Steve Kaufman/Corbis; 24 (TL, BR) Brand X Pictures; 25 (TR) Image Quest 3-D/NHPA Limited, (BR) ©OSF/Animals Animals/Earth Scenes, ©David Muench/

Corbis; 26 ©George D. Lepp/Corbis; 28 (CL, BL) Matthew Ward/©DK Images, (T) Hemera Technologies; 29 ©Klein/Hubert/Peter Arnold, Inc.; 30 (BR) ©Pat O'Hara/Corbis, (TR) ©Richard Hamilton Smith/Corbis, (TL, CL, CC, CR) ©DK Images; 31 (TR) ©DK Images, (CL) ©Roy Rainford/Robert Harding Picture Library, Ltd.; 32 (BL) Getty Images, (TL, CL) Hunt Institute for Botanical Documentation/Carnegie Mellon University, Pittsburgh, PA; **Chapter 2:** 33 (C) Tom Brakefield/Corbis, (CR) Brand X Pictures; 34 (BL) ©Don Enger/Animals Animals/Earth Scenes, (TC) ©Alan G. Nelson/Animals Animals/Earth Scenes, (BR) Getty Images; 35 (CR) ©Tom Brakefield/Corbis, (TR) ©Joe McDonald/Corbis, (BR) ©Buddy Mays/Corbis, (BL) ©Jean-Louis Le Moigne/NHPA Limited; 37 (Bkgd) ©Alan G. Nelson/Animals Animals/Earth Scenes, (TR) Brand X Pictures, (CL) ©Breck P. Kent/Animals Animals/Earth Scenes, (BCL) ©Joe McDonald/Animals Animals/Earth Scenes; 38 ©Alan G. Nelson/Animals Animals/Earth Scenes; 39 (BR) ©W. Perry Conway/Corbis, (TL) ©DK Images; 40 (BL) ©Joe McDonald/Corbis, (BC) ©George D.Lepp/Corbis, (BR) Getty Images, (TL) Hemera Technologies; 41 (BL) Getty Images, (BR) ©Tom Brakefield/Corbis; 42 (BL) ©Royalty-Free/Corbis, (TR) ©Joe McDonald/Corbis, (TL) Getty Images, ©D. Robert & Lorri Franz/Corbis; 43 ©Breck P. Kent/Animals Animals/Earth Scenes; 44 (TR) ©Jean-Louis Le Moigne/NHPA Limited, (B) ©Kent Wood/Photo Researchers, Inc., (TL) ©DK Images; 45 ©DK Images; 46 (CR, BL) ©DK Images, (TL) ©Comstock; 47 (TR, CR) ©DK Images; 48 (C) ©Stephen Dalton/NHPA Limited, (BL) ©Daniel Heuclin/NHPA Limited, (TL) Hemera Technologies; 49 ©Zig Leszczynski/Animals Animals/Earth Scenes; 50 (B) ©Carmela Leszczynski/Animals Animals/Earth Scenes, (TL) Hemera Technologies; 51 (CL) Getty Images, (C) ©Kim Taylor/Bruce Coleman Collection; 52 (TL, C) ©DK Images, (BL) ©Geoff Moon/Frank Lane Picture Agency/Corbis; 53 ©OSF/D. Clyne/Animals Animals/Earth Scenes; 54 (TL, C) ©DK Images; 55 (CR) ©Niall Benvie/Corbis, (TR, CR)©DK Images; 56 ©Dale Sanders/Masterfile Corporation; 58 (C, BC, BR) ©DK Images, (BL) ©Royalty-Free/Corbis, (CL) ©Carmela Leszczynski/Animals Animals/Earth Scenes; 59 (BL) ©DK Images, (BR) ©Daniel Heuclin/NHPA Limited; 60 (TR, CL, BR) Getty Images, (TL) ©Tom Brakefield/Corbis, (TCL) ©DK Images, (TCR) ©Joe McDonald/Corbis, (CR) ©Don Enger/Animals Animals/Earth Scenes; 61 (TR) ©DK Images, (CL, CR) Hemera Technologies; 62 (Bkgd) Map Resources, (C) ©Marian Bacon/Animals Animals/Earth Scenes, (B) Getty Images; 63 (TR) ©Andrew Syred/Photo Researchers, Inc., (T)©Royalty-Free/Corbis, (BR) MFSC/NASA, (C) ©Orbital Sciences Corporation/Photo Researchers, Inc.; 64 (BL) ©Niall Benvie/Corbis, (CL)©George Grall/National Geographic/Getty Images, (TR) ©Raymond Gehman/NGS Image Collection; **Chapter 3:** 65 (TC) ©Nigel J. Dennis/NHPA Limited, (TR) Getty Images; 66 (TC) ©Clem Haagner/Gallo Images/Corbis, (B) ©Kennan Ward/Corbis; 67 (BR) ©Randy Morse/Animals Animals/Earth Scenes, (CR) ©Stephen Frink/Corbis, (BR) ©James Watt/Animals Animals/Earth Scenes, (CR) ©Steve Bein/Corbis, (CR) ©Andrew J. Martinez/Photo Researchers, Inc., (TR) ©Sanford/Agliolo/Corbis, (TR) ©Amos Nachoum/Corbis; 69 (Bkgd) ©Clem Haagner/Gallo Images/Corbis, (TR) Getty Images; 70 Clem Haagner/Gallo Images/Corbis; 71 (R) ©Peter Johnson/Corbis, (TR) Hemera Technologies; 72 (TL) Getty Images, (B) ©Clem Haagner/Gallo Images/Corbis; 73 ©Ian Beames/Ecoscene/Corbis; 74 (BL) ©Royalty-Free/Corbis, (BR) ©Joe McDonald/Corbis, (TL) Frank Greenaway/©DK Images; 75 (BR) ©William Bernard/Corbis, ©Gaoil Shumway/Getty Images, (CR) ©Royalty-Free/Corbis; 76 (TR) ©DK Images, (TL, CR) ©Joe McDonald/Corbis, (BR) ©Stephen Krasemann/NHPA Limited, (CL)©Royalty-Free/Corbis; 77 (CL) ©Gaoil Shumway/Getty Images, (TC) ©Jim Zipp/Photo Researchers, Inc.; 78 (CL) ©Randy Morse/Animals Animals/Earth Scenes, (BC) ©Stephen Frink/Corbis, (CR) ©Andrew J. Martinez/Photo Researchers, Inc., (TL) Brand X Pictures; 79 ©Kennan Ward/Corbis; 80 (TC) ©James Watt/Animals Animals/Earth Scenes, (BR) ©Andrew J. Martinez/Photo Researchers, Inc., (CR) ©Stephen Frink/Corbis, (CL) ©Randy Morse/Animals Animals/Earth Scenes, (TL) ©Andrew J. Martinez/Photo Researchers, Inc.; 81 (T) ©Amos Nachoum/Corbis, (CR) ©Sanford/Agliolo/Corbis, (BC) ©Steve Bein/Corbis; 82 (T) ©Sanford/Agliolo/Corbis, (BL) ©Bettmann/Corbis; 83 ©Sanford/Agliolo/Corbis; 84 (B) ©Michael and Patricia Fogden/Corbis, (TL) ©DK Images; 85 ©Fred McConnaughey/Photo Researchers, Inc.; 86 (BL) ©Darrell Gulin/Corbis, (TL) Getty Images, (BR) ©Farrell Grehan/Corbis; 87 ©DK Images; 88 (CL) ©Pete Atkinson/NHPA Limited, (TL) NHPA Limited; 89 (CC) ©Eric and David Hosking/Corbis, (TC) ©Rob C. Nunnington/Gallo Images/Corbis, (TR) ©Richard Murphy; 90 ©Kennan Ward/Corbis; 92 (TR) ©Joe McDonald/Corbis, (BR) ©D. Robert and Lorri Franz/Corbis, (BL) Frank Greenaway/©DK Images, (Bkgd) ©William Manning/Corbis, (BL) Getty Images, (CL) Jane Burton/©DK Images; 94 (BR) ©Clem Haagner/Gallo Images/Corbis, (TC) ©Stephen Krasemann/NHPA Limited, (TR) ©Randy Morse/Animals Animals/Earth Scenes, (CL, CR) ©Royalty-Free/Corbis, (C) ©Joe McDonald/Corbis; 95 (CL) ©George H. H. Huey/Corbis, (CR) ©Norbert Rosing/NGS Image Collection, (TR) ©Andrew J. Martinez/Photo Researchers, Inc.; 96